Gathering Years

How to Grow Old without

Killing Yourself

Terrie Carpenter, PT

Specialist in pain management and sustainable recovery

Gathering Years

How to Grow Old without Killing Yourself

Terrie Carpenter

Print ISBN: 978-1-54393-367-3

eBook ISBN: 978-1-54393-368-0

Table of Contents

Part 1: Setting the Foundation 1

Welcome to My World 1

Aging: A Different Perspective 4

The Unavoidable Downward Cycle 6

Treat Yourself Like Your Own Best Friend! 7

The Change Model 8

One More Thing to Remember 12

Part 2: Strategies on How to Grow Old without Killing Yourself 14

Stay Hydrated 15

Implement "Protein Washing" 17

Move as If Your Life Depended on It (Because It Does!) 19

Use All of Your Real Estate Every Day 21

Worship Your Feet 23

Stand tall 25

Challenge Your Balance 28

Use Your Core During All Your Movements 30

Pay Attention to Your Strength Daily 32

Learn to Pace Your Activities 34

Loosen Gravity's Grip: De-Weight Yourself   37

Develop Good Sleep Hygiene Practices   39

Experience Delight!   41

Part 3: Conclusion   43

What About Pain?   43

Toward a New Beginning   45

Part 1: Setting the Foundation

Welcome to My World

How do you define aging? What does aging mean to you?

In the normative world, aging is defined as the final phase of life, filled with pain, negativity, and limitations. Some of the synonyms for *aging* include *crumbling, declining, fading, fermenting, slumping, becoming stale, waning, and wearing out.*

That's not my world. My world is a world of possibilities and opportunities, of wisdom and experience. My world is a world where aging is a bountiful accumulation of years and experiences, full of stories and a plethora of successes, mistakes, and lessons learned along the way. In my world, the word *vibrant* means *active, dynamic, energetic, spirited, vigorous, animated, sparkling, vivacious,* and *passionate*; here *graceful* means *limber, lithe, rhythmic, symmetrical, easy, elastic, poised, practiced,* and *flowing.* Welcome to *my world.* Wouldn't you like it to be your world too?

My hope in writing this book is to change the definitions and dialogue that surround the process of aging, or what I like to call *gathering years.* I am excited to share with you what I have learned about "growing old without killing yourself."

I bring to this book almost fifty years of clinical experience in the field of physical therapy and pain management. I am blessed to still be practicing in my field as a respected pain management specialist in the San Francisco Bay Area.

Even though I have been at it for many years, I am still fascinated with the work that I do. Although I am into my seventies, my life and my own aging process still fascinate and inspire me as well.

As my seventieth birthday approached, I was clear that I wanted to celebrate it with every cell in my body (you're going to come across many references to cells in this book)! From zip lining through Sonoma County to dancing under the stars at Coit Tower in San Francisco, that is just what I did—grandly celebrating the gathering of another year.

Throughout my life, I have exercised and remained relatively fit, but as I turned seventy, I wanted to explore the boundaries of my physical fitness and challenge my physical self in a new way and see how much stronger and even more fit I might become. I signed up for a very intense and vigorous exercise class called Pure Barre. Even though I have been in the business of helping others reach their optimal physical capacity levels for half a century, I was surprised and amazed by what my body could still learn. The strength, balance, endurance, and sense of well-being that I have gained through this class is stunning.

I am not necessarily recommending that it's right for everyone to join a vigorous exercise class, but I do want to impress upon you how much the body and brain can still learn at any age. I also want to gently remind you that regardless of your current fitness level, you can always improve, get stronger and more flexible, or have better balance and posture.

What this will require is changing some habits on your part. It's critical to understand that changing is a *process*, not an event, and must be honored as so. Practically speaking, humans change slowly and reach sustainable change only by taking small incremental steps and by doing things consistently to develop new habits.

"How to Grow Old without Killing Yourself" is a collection of my personal and professional reflections and observations on how to make the aging process feel more gentle, more graceful, less painful, and more fun!

I hope you enjoy this book and find the content thought provoking, inspiring, and possibly even a little transformational in the way you negotiate your own aging process.

Please remember:

- You are never too old to change!
- You are never too old to get in better shape!
- You are never too old to laugh and to live in abundance!

Be courageous!

Terrie Carpenter

Aging: A Different Perspective

Some would have us believe the aging process comes with the absolute certainty of pain, immobility, decreased brain agility, depression, and general unhappiness.

Consider the following two questions:

- Are you afraid of the aging process?
- Would you like to have a positive impact on your own aging process?

As I reflect on my private practice, it is clear to me that much of the suffering I have witnessed in the aging population could have been lessened significantly. It also occurred to me in the most startling way that our culture treats the aging process like it treats chronic pain: with dangerous medications, destabilizing procedures, and imposed limitations.

Furthermore, it is common for people in pain to think they should not move in order to avoid further pain. It is also common for older people to think they should stay still for fear of falling. To be clear, this decrease in activity worsens pain and hastens aging. Simply put, it's time to shift the paradigm.

As a pain management specialist, I collaborate with my clients and support them in making the positive and lasting changes necessary to reach their optimal health. Nowhere is this collaboration more important than it is when one is dealing with the aging population.

I fully understand that our genetics play an important role in our individual experience of aging. However, my personal and professional experience has convinced me that we have more control over the quality of our aging experience than commonly thought.

The aging process starts in our cells. Our cells change and, in a sense, they wear out. It is also the job of our cells to constantly restore themselves. I believe it is our job as individuals to live in a way that creates the best possible environment in our bodies for our cells to live and restore. Any healing or anti-aging process must start at the cellular level. These cellular restoration practices are what I call good self-care!

We can sit down and let the aging process have its way with us. Or, we can consciously and mindfully decide how we will live from moment to moment as if our lives depended on it—because in reality, they absolutely do!

To be clear, we can *choose* to practice careless deterioration, or we can choose to practice mindful restoration to the best of our abilities.

The Unavoidable Downward Cycle

Here is a simple, raw truth: The more you sit, the weaker you get; the weaker you get, the more you fall; the more you fall, the more fearful you get; the more fearful you become, the smaller your world gets. Then you sit in a chair and wait to die!

Just about everything we do today hastens the process of cellular devastation. We sit too much, we use technology too much, we live with high levels of stress, and we are constantly running around. We often attempt to put a positive spin on our overcommitted lives. Relaxation is viewed as unproductive. We tend to have no restorative downtime.

This exhausting and draining combination of behaviors hastens the aging process by sending our nervous system into overdrive (who hasn't heard of "burnout?"), making our cells more vulnerable.

Self-care has the opposite effect: it keeps our nervous system calm and promotes renewal and regeneration of our cells. We develop cellular resilience to the fluctuations in our basic physiology.

When we are healthy, grounded, and calm, our mind, body, and spirit work as an integrated system. We are conscious and aware of when we are tired, stressed, fatigued, or in pain.

This awareness enables us to take affirmative action toward restoring ourselves. That is the process I call true self-care.

Treat Yourself Like Your Own Best Friend!

When I see new clients, I often ask them in their first visit who the most treasured person in their life might be. Then I ask them if they would treat that person with the same harshness as they treat themselves. Consistently, the answer is no!

We all know that we are supposed to take good care of ourselves. Why then does it seem so difficult to do? Because we bite off more than we can chew and make it too darned hard on ourselves. And, as I mentioned earlier, change is a process, not an event!

Unfortunately, we live in a quick fix/instant change culture. We are told every day to "just do it." Every magazine you read speaks of a new youth-promoting, weight loss, anti-aging, body-sculpting system—that will, of course, work in eight days. Quick change is a myth; it takes us down a sure road to failure, self-judgment, and feelings of shame.

Human beings change slowly, by taking one small step at a time. This concept is so critical that I've developed a specific framework called the Change Model. I use this model in my private practice because it clearly addresses the human process of creating lasting and sustainable change.

The Change Model

With the goal of becoming a healthier and more vibrant person (with happy, restoring cells), let's take a look at the Change Model. It will empower you to make the changes you desire gently and successfully so that you can *grow old without killing yourself.*

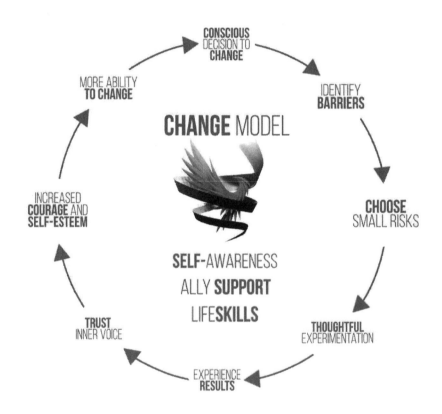

When attempting to form new habits, people generally don't understand this concept: When you decide to make a change, every reason you have ever had for not making that change comes to the surface. In other words, all of your past attempts, all of your fears, and all of your self-limiting beliefs take front and center. These are your barriers.

Examples of personal barriers

- My habits are hardwired.
- I'm actually afraid.
- I don't have time to do anything else.
- I don't feel well enough.
- I hurt.
- I wouldn't know where to start.
- I can't afford a gym membership.
- I feel embarrassed about my body.
- I'm too old.
- I feel overwhelmed by all the information out there.
- I don't know what my doctor would say.
- Nothing ever works for me.
- Add your own . . .

These barriers need to be identified and resolved so that you can move forward in your process of change. However, simply identifying them in your own head and attempting to find a solution alone generally does not work.

In my practice and personal experience, I see how people are better able to identify and address their barriers with the help of another person. This is what I refer to as Ally Support.

Since I am usually the first ally that my clients encounter, I will model the Ally process to my clients beginning with our first interaction. All of my interactions with clients will be collaborative, non-shaming, and nonjudgmental. This enables my clients to feel good about themselves and to focus on the changes they are interested in making. That is the hallmark of Ally Support*.

Don't be afraid to ask someone to be your ally. The most important quality to look for in an ally is that, at the end of every interaction, you feel really good about yourself. If you feel shame, blame, or guilt, he or she is not the right person.

You deserve communication, support, and collaboration that are

- Nonjudgmental
- Non-shaming
- Safe
- Consistent
- Able to meet and accept you where you are
- Respectful
- Self-esteem raising
- Collaborative

There is an added benefit to Ally Support because as people age they tend to isolate and shrink their worlds. Allies for the aging population are therefore extremely beneficial and even imperative.

In viewing the Change Model again, with your solid Ally Support backing you up, you will also see it is important to start with an action that you are actually able to follow through with. This is how you build the "change muscle," one small step and one small success at a time.

Again, drastic changes are not required or even preferred. Begin with one of the simple self-care practices detailed in this book and incorporate it into your "already life." What is your already life, you might ask? Think of it this way: you already live twenty-four hours a day. You already have a routine that you generally follow in those twenty-four hours. It can be easy to insert some small, new practices into that existing twenty-four hours rather than attempt to reorganize your entire life.

For example, you might want to start walking every morning five to seven days a week while simultaneously and drastically changing your diet. In my experience, a combined decision such as this will end in failure because the goal was much too big to begin with.

In my private practice, I like to collaborate with my clients to come up with a more realistic first step, because I know that success breeds more success. So I might ask them, "Instead of walking every morning this week, what do you think about starting by walking one time this week and drinking one more glass of water a day than you do currently? Does that feel like something you are comfortable committing to?"

Success with this small change will help you build up to the next small change, and the next small change, eventually adding up to your end desired result: the full transformation.

One More Thing to Remember

Our patterns of behavior are hardwired into our brains and our nervous systems. We unconsciously keep repeating them. Change requires an interruption of those patterns so that we become more conscious about our actions.

One of the most effective pattern interruption techniques I use in my practice is to set up a texting pattern with clients. It can be as simple as sending an emoji or a one-word text indicating successful follow-through. If my client doesn't send the first text, then I initiate the text or call. (If you are not someone who texts, a brief phone call or voice mail message can achieve the same effect.) It is this interruption that will reinforce new behavior in the beginning.

Baby steps to pattern interruption:

- Make a gold star chart, put it on your refrigerator, and add a star each time you are successful. It is surprising how good you feel watching those stars accumulate.

- Leave a one-word voice mail message with your ally.

- Add a new accessory (like a bracelet or hair tie) to your wrist so that when you look down you are reminded about your new action.

- Put a small reminder note in a place you go to all the time (like the bathroom or a mirror).

- Link your new habit to a bit of music and then play the music often.

- Visualize yourself doing the new habit frequently.

- Use a television commercial to remember to stretch.

- Get creative with your pattern interrupters and have fun.

Part 2: Strategies on How to Grow Old without Killing Yourself

I hope that I've given you a new perspective on how you can actually make the changes you desire. Now, let's look at some specific techniques and strategies that you can begin to incorporate in your life. I hope you can look at these suggestions with some joy at what possibilities are in store for you. You are never too old to change. In fact, change is one of the things that keep us open-minded, open-hearted, and alive.

Choose one small step to begin. When you are consistently successful with that step, you can go back to the list and add one more small thing, all the while increasing your ability to create sustaining habit change.

Stay Hydrated

Why? Dehydration is one of the great enemies of the aging population. It leads to many health risks. Cells that don't maintain their balance of fluids and electrolytes shrivel. This can result in muscle fatigue, general weakness, unclear thinking, and so forth.

When muscle cells don't have adequate fluids, they don't work as well. This dehydration contributes to the progressive muscle weakness found in the more mature population. The same can be said of brain cells. Simply put, dehydration compounds the aging process.

It is very important to find your own hydration style. For example, I will never stay hydrated by remembering to go to the sink, fill up a glass, and drink it multiple times a day. I also know that I have to drink out of a straw. To that end, I have created my own "adult sippy cup": a tall plastic cup with a lid, insulated sleeve, and a straw. It is always with me when appropriate. I know if I fill it three times a day I have met my hydration goals. For me, adding a splash of Light Cran-Raspberry juice helps it go down more easily.

Baby steps to hydration

- Find a satisfactory reusable water container.
- Drink one glass of water when you get up.
- Drink one glass of water when you drink your coffee.
- Set the timer on your watch or other electronic device to remind you when to drink a glass of water.
- Text a friend or ally each time you drink a glass.

- Have your friend/ally text you if they haven't heard from you.

- Add a splash of juice, iced tea, or some fresh herbs like mint to liven up your water.

- Commit with your ally/buddy.

- Talk to friends, co-workers, or anybody, really, about your new goal to drink more water.

Once you manage to remain hydrated for a period of time, you will want to take all the necessary measures to avoid any future chances of dehydration. You will think more clearly, you will feel more vibrant, and your "change muscle" will be stronger!

Implement "Protein Washing"

Why? Protein is good for building and maintaining your muscles and bones despite the aging process; it's also important for strength and function. The body converts protein into muscle.

Eating protein evenly throughout the day greatly enhances this process. When you spread your protein intake evenly throughout the day, your muscles receive a constant supply of the amino acids needed to build muscle and boost metabolism.

In our culture, we tend to eat too little protein at breakfast and too much at dinner. Our bodies can't build muscle throughout the day, and are forced to oxidize and store protein as glucose or fat at night.

In my practice I recommend the two–three strategy: graze on small portions of protein every two to three hours throughout the day. Your energy levels will be more stable, you won't experience as many highs and lows, and your cravings for sugar will also decrease. You will feel stronger and, therefore, you will be less likely to fall down!

Baby steps to protein washing

- Educate yourself about protein! This does not have to involve extensive research (although it is fascinating to look at this in depth). Try googling "simple sources of protein."

- Buy a whole roasted chicken and eat little bits of it throughout the day/week.

- Buy a small personal cooler so you never leave home without your protein.

- Try cooking six hard-boiled eggs (just one example—any protein is good) for the week and put them in your cooler to eat one in the middle of the day.

- Get some small containers of chicken, tuna, egg, or bean salad to keep in your refrigerator. Having protein sources handy is really important, especially if you are busy. You don't want to get to the point where you're hungry and don't have any healthy snacks readily available.

- Have small portions of nuts easily available (carry them in your pocket or purse, or put a couple of small servings in your desk and car for those times when you are low-energy and/or having a food craving).

- Plan ahead.

- Pretend you like protein. Fake it until you make it is a real thing!

- Commit to your ally/buddy.

Eating regularly can easily translate into better health and a lasting habit that matters. You don't want to get to a certain age and not have the appetite or ability to eat, because you had so much inconsistency throughout your younger years.

Move as If Your Life Depended on It (Because It Does!)

Why? Motion keeps your joints lubricated—motion is lotion for your body parts. A body at rest tends to stay at rest; a body in motion keeps moving. Without question, the biggest risk factor in the aging population is decreased activity and mobility.

I like to have my clients think of movement rather than exercise. Tell people they have to exercise and watch them automatically shut down. The exercise world has gone crazy; and with the new obsession to look and be fit at the cost of other important self-care techniques, many people feel excluded, disregarded, or simply unable to meet the standards of fitness.

No one mentions that just the act of moving on a regular basis will benefit your body, mind, and spirit more than you can imagine. We don't all have to be bikini models, professional athletes, or marathon runners and triathlon contestants; we can simply be relatively active and engaged in movement. In my collaboration with other practitioners in the medical community, we all repeatedly agree that movement is life-giving and life-saving.

Baby steps to becoming a body in motion

- Forget the gym. Walk through the available space in your house a few times a day.
- When you stand up from a chair, stand up twice.
- Get down on the floor and get up every day.

- Roll over on your stomach every day.

- Set a timer so you don't sit any longer than forty-five minutes without moving or stretching.

- Put on some music and move to the beat.

- Do five to ten mini-squats while you brush your teeth.

- Commit with your ally/buddy.

A body in motion can stay in motion. A body that sits too long can't even get up. Remember, change breeds change!

Use All of Your Real Estate Every Day

Why? Nowhere is the saying "use it or lose it" more applicable than in reference to the human body. Allow me to introduce you to your fascia and to "shrink-wrap syndrome."

Fascia is a thin membranous layer of tissue that lies under the skin. It is what would hold us together if our skin were peeled away. It is one continuous structure that exists from our head to our fingertips to the tips of our toes. It also wraps around our organs. Think of it this way: we all have our own personal sausage casing. That is how all the parts of our body are connected and interdependent.

Shrink-wrap syndrome refers to fascial restrictions that can cause an array of problems, such as pain, headaches, digestive distress, decreased mobility, postural deformity, walking distress, decreased flexibility, and reduced stability. Furthermore, these restrictions become a major contributor to the increased difficulty seniors have in performing their daily activities. This decreased mobility adds to the anxiety that so many older people already feel in their daily life.

Shrink-wrap syndrome can be avoided and even reversed (to a degree) by moving all of your muscles and joints frequently. Moving frequently doesn't mean you have to join an exercise class; you can do this in small increments throughout your "already day." The one thing to avoid at all costs is prolonged sitting. That shriveled-up, shuffling movement we see in so many older people is absolutely unnecessary!

Move anything you can. Movement keeps us open and juicy!

Baby steps to moving your "real estate"

- Change your position often.
- Reach for the sky, especially if you are sitting a lot.
- Straighten one leg at a time while sitting (you want to feel that nice stretch in the back of your leg).
- Lie down on your bed and stretch out to your full length daily.
- Look up, look down, look side to side.
- Give yourself a big hug.
- Pretend you are typing or playing the piano.
- Take a deep breath whenever you think about it (not only does it help your lungs and your brain, but it is good for all the little joints in your spine).
- Take a few minutes to look closely at your body and notice all of your movable parts. Then move one of them through its entire range of motion, then another, and another.

Remember, humans are designed to move at all ages!

Worship Your Feet

Why? Your feet are so important they deserve their own section. If you only do one thing as result of reading this book, do this: Keep your feet flexible and strong.

The foundation for all of our upright movement is our feet. One of the most common problems I see in my older clients is that they have feet like bricks: stiff, hard, and immobile.

Feet that are stiff and immovable lead to decreased mobility, poor posture, poor balance, and painful and effortful walking. It is easy to feel off-balance when your feet are stiff. If you feel off-balance, you are more likely to fall; then you will become more fearful to move much at all.

Keep in mind that you have all of the joints and muscles in your feet that you have in your hands (except the opposable thumb). Nowhere is shrink-wrap syndrome more evident and more dangerous than in our feet.

Baby steps to worshiping your feet

- Stand in bare feet and see if all of your toes can touch the ground. If they don't, choose one of the actions below.
- If you are sitting in a chair, take off your shoes, look at your toes, and wiggle, wiggle, wiggle them!
- Point your toes away from you and then pull them toward you.
- Roll your feet around on a tennis ball.

- If you get out of the tub or shower and you sit down to dry your toes, pull on them and bend them.

- At some point during the day when you are standing, roll forward on your toes and then lean back on your heels.

- Wear good, supportive shoes often. Purchase shoes that don't smash your toes together and ones that have adequate cushion.

- Buy insoles for your shoes if needed. Some of the over-the-counter ones are a great place to start.

- If you can reach your feet, massage them lovingly with lotion.

- Get regular pedicures (or massages), if possible. This applies to men as well as women!

Remember to give thanks for your feet because without them you will go nowhere.

Stand tall

Why? Have you noticed that many older adults (and some younger) have developed a kind of forward stooping posture? This deterioration process is often taken for granted and accepted as a natural progression of the aging process. As your body begins to stoop over, destabilizing changes occur with your balance and center of gravity. Over time, this stooping position makes you more unstable as you walk and, coupled with stiff feet, dramatically increases your chances of falling.

In addition, adaptive patterns of movement can increase the stress on your joints and wear them out prematurely. For instance, a slouching posture compresses your spine. This can lead to more rapid degeneration of your discs and ultimately result in a kind of chronic pain.

Conversely, good posture makes you feel better. Your muscles are more limber, and you have better mobility and less tension in your neck, shoulders, back, legs, and spine. Thus, having a good posture is very important to preventing pain and maintaining better balance.

Once an individual's posture has deteriorated to the point you see replicated in the diagram below, that person is much more vulnerable to falls and poor health. You can see that the center of gravity is shifted forward and the shrink-wrap process has taken over.

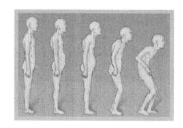

It isn't hard to imagine that the forward stooping posture you see here can result in pain, stiffness, decreased general mobility, and weakness while increasing the fear of moving around.

Besides, this posture makes people look, feel, and act old. Yet it can so easily be prevented.

Baby steps for standing tall

- When you're walking, look at the horizon, not at the ground below you.
- Every time you stand up, stand up as tall as you can.
- Stand up once for every half hour that you sit.
- Look at yourself in a mirror and notice your posture.
- Stand with your back against the wall and lift your back and shoulders up.
- Take deep breaths.
- Stretch your fingertips to the sky whenever you think about it.
- Notice people with good posture and try to copy them.
- Get out of your chair every chance you get.
- Smile! When people smile it often automatically improves their posture.

And remember, no matter how old you are, it is never too late to improve your posture!

Challenge Your Balance

Why? According to the Centers for Disease Control, "each year, millions of older people—those 65 and older—fall. In fact, one out of three older people falls each year, but less than half tell their doctor. Falling once doubles your chances of falling again." Falls and fall-related injuries, such as hip fracture, can have a serious impact on an older person's life.

A fall could limit your activities or make it impossible to live independently. Balance plays a key role in fall prevention. Too often, the first encounter an older person has with balance training occurs after he or she has fallen and sustained an injury. Those injuries can often be prevented with good balance.

Balance is your ability to maintain your center of gravity over your base of support. When you're standing up, your legs are your base of support. The wider your stance is, the wider your base is and the easier it is to balance. The closer together your legs are, the narrower your base of support and the harder it is to remain balanced.

Balance also means that you can evenly distribute your weight, enabling you to remain upright and steady. Balance can be practiced and strengthened, thereby becoming one of the most important tools you can have to prevent falls and injury. Generally speaking, the more movement you make, the more balance you'll create. Oh darn, there's that movement thing again. Do you see an organizing principle of movement in all of this?

Baby steps for challenging your balance

- Stand still with your feet about ten inches apart and your belly button pulled toward your back. Count to ten, then twenty, then thirty.

- Now do it with your eyes closed.

- Now do it on one foot, then the other.

- Do it in the grocery line.

- Do it while you are brushing your teeth.

- Walk backward.

- Walk sideways.

- Learn to dance.

- Learn tai chi.

- Practice shifting your weight from one side to another.

- Stand up from a chair (or the floor) without using your hands.

- Sit on a stability ball.

Use Your Core During All Your Movements

Why? Strong core muscles make it easier to do everything from swinging a golf club to growing older. Good balance and a strong core go hand in hand. Weak core muscles leave you susceptible to poor posture, lower back pain, muscle injuries, and a decreased ability to carry out your daily activities.

Your core is a complex series of muscles, extending far beyond your abdominals, including everything besides your arms and legs. It needs to be engaged in almost every movement of the human body. Think of it like a corset that encases your body's torso.

Your core is the stabilizing part of your body that helps keeps all of your daily movements safe and free from injury. Maintaining a strong body core is important at any age. It is critical as we get older, and no one tells us that or teaches us how.

As people age they sit more. This unfortunately leads to a combination of tight postural muscles and a weak core. This combination leaves us vulnerable to injury at any age. It can become deadly as we reach our senior years, because it puts more strain on every body part from our feet to our lower back to our neck.

So do we need to hire a trainer or join a gym or a fitness class? The answer is no, not to get started!

Baby steps for calling on your core

- Breathe in through your nose and out against gently pursed lips. Prolong that breath out and, as you do, imagine pulling your belly button toward your back, lacing your corset.
- Lace your corset (engage your core)
  - during each commercial on TV.
  - during each stop light that you encounter while driving or riding in a car.
  - while brushing your teeth.
  - when taking your laundry out of the dryer.
  - when you blow your nose.
  - when you put the dishes in the cupboard.
- When you walk, imagine lengthening your entire body.
- Think *glide* instead of *walk*.

There is a psychological benefit to having a strong core, because you tend to feel safe in your body; and when you feel safe in your body, you will naturally move more.

Pay Attention to Your Strength Daily

Why? Strength training done regularly not only builds up bone and muscle but also counteracts the weakness and frailty that usually come with aging. Any strength that you build or maintain keeps you feeling safer in your body and less likely to fall.

Strength training also helps reduce the signs and symptoms of many assumed age-related disorders like

- Osteoporosis
- Heart disease
- Obesity
- Back pain
- Joint pain
- Depression
- Anxiety

To maintain or improve your strength, must you join a gym or take a vigorous exercise class? No, not necessarily.

Keep in mind that this book is about *simple interventions* that you can easily add to your "already life." When you have been mindful about your fitness level for a while, you might naturally want to add something more vigorous to your plan, but it is not necessary.

Baby steps to keeping your strength up

- When you stand up from a chair, stand up twice.

- At every TV commercial, straighten each leg ten times (if you are sitting).

- Lift some soup cans while you engage your core.

- Put your hands on the wall in front of you and do some wall push-ups.

- Rise up on your tiptoes a few times while you are brushing your teeth.

- March in place while you engage your core.

- As you carry grocery bags, bend your elbows to strengthen your biceps.

- Pull on elastic exercise bands while you watch TV.

- Get creative and use your imagination to work on your strength.

You are never too old to get stronger! Remember the exercise class I mentioned that I joined on my seventieth birthday? After many months of consistent attendance (first three times a week and eventually four), I am much stronger. Even as a health professional with good knowledge, I was shocked myself at how much more I could grow, learn, change, and become stronger.

Learn to Pace Your Activities

Why? Pacing your activity throughout the day will decrease your stress levels, restore your cells, and make day-to-day living more pleasant in general. We all understand the money/budget concept: if you spend it all at the first of the month, the rest of the month requires deprivation and risking having a bank account in the red.

Your energy stores are your personal living bank account. You can spend the resources all at once in a grand manner, and then struggle to find the energy to keep going, or you can budget your energy output to last longer.

I like to offer this metaphor to the individuals who work with me. Think of yourself as an ATM. If you drive by many times a day to withdraw money but you never drive by to deposit money, you will eventually become bankrupt. Our bodies and health follow the same principle. We need a balance of deposits and withdrawals—deposits of good self-care and withdrawals of energy needed for all our daily activities—but we need to be mindful of excessive energy withdrawals.

Examples of excessive withdrawals:

- Saying yes when we want to say no to requests for our time
- Overcommitting in general
- Getting dehydrated
- Staying dehydrated
- Going without breakfast

- Eating while you are standing
- Going too long without protein
- Having no downtime away from technical devices
- Chronically multitasking
- Sitting many hours a day
- Living life in a constant state of stress
- Rushing

In our culture, we are drawn to the "spend it all at once" concept. It's like fireworks: big, bright, and exciting but fizzling out quickly, leaving nothing as a backup. This practice of going big and then crashing down is costly to our cells. Give conscious attention to pacing habits in order to balance your accounts.

Baby steps to pacing your activities

- When you drive somewhere and you reach your destination, take three deep breaths before you get out of the car.
- Set an intention for how you want your day to go before you even get out of bed.
- Notice the color of the sky.
- Slow down.
- Speak more slowly.
- Sit down when you eat. Consider using a placemat and a linen napkin even if you are eating alone.
- Avoid eating while doing other things (like working at your desk).

- Smile at the checker in the grocery store.

- Practice random gratitude.

Loosen Gravity's Grip: De-Weight Yourself

Why? This practice is ridiculously simple and effective. By *de-weight*, I mean lie down. I also call this the "body sigh." Loosening gravity's grip on your body for even a couple of minutes is unbelievably restorative.

Gravity is fantastic (or we would all be floating out in space). But it does take a toll on our systems. It literally pulls everything down and compresses us. Gravity can contribute to the dreaded shrink-wrap syndrome.

I challenge you to give regular de-weighting a try and notice how you feel. Do not talk on your phone while de-weighting. This is *downtime*. You will most likely notice that you can breathe more easily and you will experience refreshing of your energy.

I am talking about doing this for just a few minutes a few times a day. You can do this in your car if need be. Just put the seat all the way back. If you have no place to stretch out at work, at least do it as you transition to home.

Baby steps to loosening gravity's grip

- Stretch out on the floor and put your lower legs up on a chair.
- Stretch out on your bed with a couple of pillows under your knees.
- Put the seat all the way back in your car and stretch out.

- If you are at work and can't lie down, at least do this: stand up, reach for your toes, then straighten up and reach for the sky. This action will decompress you a little and get your muscles moving).

Develop Good Sleep Hygiene Practices

Why? You often hear people say that sleep gets more difficult as we age; yet sleep continues to be one of the most restorative parts of our lives. It is worth spending a little time and effort to make sleep a successful experience.

Please note that everything I have suggested to you so far in terms of self-care can be considered as sleep hygiene. Good sleep hygiene practices can prevent the development of sleep problems.

If you are experiencing sleep problems, it's a good idea to evaluate your sleep routine. Please don't assume that *just because you are aging* you won't sleep well. Not true!

Baby steps to good sleep hygiene

- Start with one thing that I have suggested in terms of self-care.
- In the hour before you go to sleep, change your environment in some way:

    Dim the lights.

    Light some flameless candles.

    Place a moist heat pack on your chest.

    Take a break from all electronic equipment.

    Make your bed deliciously cozy.

- Do some gentle stretching.

- Notice your breathing.

- Figure out what your most comfortable sleeping position might be.

- Turn off your phone and stop looking at electronic screens for at least 30 minutes before sleeping.

Experience Delight!

Why? I have the privilege and delight of spending a good bit of time with my two-year-old grandson. He is so in the moment that he notices everything with great delight. Today he picked a lemon off a tree. He examined at it so carefully. He smelled it and broke into a smile. Then when I handed him a thin slice of the lemon and he tasted it, he puckered up with great surprise.

This sense of wonder and delight is like a muscle—unused it will shrink and get weak. For some reason as we gather years, we slowly disconnect with the small wonders that are around us all the time. Unfortunately, the more we disconnect, the more brittle and dry we become. I am encouraging you to reclaim your sense of wonder and delight. It will keep you juicy!

Baby steps to experiencing delight

- Find a two-year-old child to mimic.
- Smell a lemon.
- Laugh from your belly.
- Write a gratitude list when you can.
- Notice your fascinating toes.
- Learn a new word.
- Learn a new skill.
- Lie on your back in the grass and see the color of the sky.
- Make stories up about the cloud shapes.

- Try a new taste sensation.

- Move your body with abandon.

- Feel your breath.

- Notice how a certain sound feels on your tongue.

- Love with all your being.

- And so many more—use your imagination and discover your own delights.

Part 5: Conclusion

What About Pain?

Please don't assume that pain is the indicator that something awful is wrong with you. I am not talking about broken-leg pain here. I'm talking about the daily aches and pains we often associate with the aging process.

I challenge you to think of those aches and pains as your friends. Those sensations are often alerting you that something in your body is out of balance. Your fascia may be shrink-wrapped and your joints may be compressed. Those sensations can be your body's attempt to get your attention and remind you to take good care of yourself.

For example, back pain does not necessarily mean that you need to sit down or go to bed. An episode of back pain is often a signal that you have been using your body incorrectly and you have allowed the shrink-wrap process to set in.

Very often back pain means we need to move more, stretch more, or drink more water. Before you go to your doctor and get pain medication, you might want to try some of the strategies I have outlined for you. If need be, get help from a practitioner who understands soft tissue disorders and can teach you the correct ways to move your body.

Taking pain medication can sometimes lead down a very dark road: First, it changes how you function in the world. Furthermore, it is very hard on your digestive system and before you know it, you are taking another medication for constipation.

It is sadly amazing how many medications we might be prescribed as we grow older. We must stay proactive in our own health care by asking questions and understanding any recommended treatment options. Taking someone with you to your doctor's appointments is a genius idea!

Toward a New Beginning

Congratulations if you have persisted to the end of this book. That means you have a real investment in changing your habits to promote your optimum health as you gather years.

It has been a genuine pleasure for me to pull all this together and share it with you as you join me on this unique and challenging adventure. It is important to me that all of the experience and knowledge I have accumulated over the years be put to good use.

It is completely possible to avoid unnecessary pain and suffering and sustain vital and vibrant lives!

With blessings and deep regards,

Terrie Carpenter

For more information on How to Grow Old
without Killing Yourself, visit

www.allies4change.com

Don't hesitate to contact me and our Allies for Change
office at (415) 454-3657 for education sessions or an
individual consultation.